Making Smart Money Through Online Tutoring 5

Chapter 1: Introduction to Online Tutoring and Teaching 5
1.1 Overview of Online Tutoring and Teaching 5
   1.1.1 Understanding Asynchronous Learning 6
   1.1.2 Benefits of Asynchronous Learning 7
   1.1.3 Challenges of Asynchronous Learning 9
   1.1.4 Strategies for Effective Asynchronous Learning 10
   1.1.5 Tools for Asynchronous Learning 11
1.2 The Growth of Online Education 13
1.3 Why Consider Online Tutoring and Teaching? 14

Chapter 2: Getting Started as an Online Tutor 15
2.1 Identifying Your Niche and Expertise 15
2.2 Essential Tools and Technologies 16
   2.2.1 Required Hardware: 17
   2.2.2 Recommended Software: 17
      2.2.2.1 Video Conferencing Tools: 17
      2.2.2.2 Learning Management Systems (LMS): 18
      2.2.2.3 Interactive Tools: 19
      2.2.2.4 Content Creation Tools: 20
      2.2.2.5 Communication Tools: 21
      2.2.2.6 Assessment Tools: 22
2.3 Setting Up Your Online Tutoring Business 22
   2.3.1 Establishing Your Brand 23
      2.3.1.1 Why Branding Matters: 23
      2.3.1.2 Steps to Establish Your Brand: 24

    2.3.1.3 Case Study: Building a Successful Online Tutoring Brand — 30

Chapter 3: Finding and Attracting Students — 31
  3.1 Choosing the Right Platforms — 31
  3.2 Marketing Yourself — 32
    3.2.1 Key Elements of an Effective Marketing Strategy: — 33
    3.2.2 Case Study: Effective Marketing for Online Tutors — 40
  3.3 Networking and Referrals — 42
    3.3.1 Networking Strategies: — 42
      3.3.1.1 Join Professional Organizations — 42
      Becoming a member of professional organizations related to education and your subject area can provide numerous benefits. — 42
      3.3.1.2 Attend Conferences and Workshops — 43
      3.3.1.3 Participate in Online Communities — 44
      3.3.1.4 Collaborate with Other Educators — 44
      3.3.1.5 Connect with Local Schools and Institutions — 45
    3.3.2 Referral Strategies — 45
      3.3.2.1 Create a Referral Program — 45
      3.3.2.2 Collect and Showcase Testimonials — 46
      3.3.2.3 Leverage Online Reviews — 46
      3.3.2.4 Utilize Email Marketing — 47
      3.3.2.5 Provide Exceptional Service — 47
      3.3.2.6 Network with Influencers and Thought Leaders — 48
      3.3.2.7 Case Study: Successful Networking and Referral Strategies — 49

Chapter 4: Creating Effective Online Courses — 51
- 4.1 Understanding Online Course Design — 51
- 4.2 Structuring Your Course Content — 53
- 4.3 Developing Engaging Multimedia Content — 54
- 4.4 Facilitating Online Discussions and Collaboration — 56
- 4.5 Assessing Student Learning Effectively — 57
- 4.6 Providing Feedback and Support — 59
- 4.7 Continuous Improvement and Evaluation — 60
- 4.8 Platforms for Hosting Courses — 62

Chapter 5: Delivering High-Quality Instruction — 64
- 5.1 Best Practices for Online Teaching — 64
- 5.2 Handling Challenges — 72
  - 5.2.1. Technological Issues: — 73
  - 5.2.2. Student Engagement and Participation: — 74
  - 5.2.3 Time Management: — 75
  - 5.2.4 Assessment Integrity — 76
  - 5.2.5 Building Community and Support — 78
  - 5.2.6 Professional Development and Adaptation — 79

Chapter 6: Scaling Your Online Tutoring Business — 81
- 6.1 Setting Strategic Goals for Scaling — 81
  - 6.1.1 Key Steps: — 81
- 6.2 Optimizing Operations for Efficiency — 84
  - 6.2.1 Operational Strategies: — 84
- 6.3 Scaling Through Strategic Partnerships — 87
  - 6.3.1 Partnership Opportunities: — 87
- 6.4 Monitoring and Evaluating Scalability — 90
  - 6.4.1 Evaluation Metrics: — 90

Chapter 7: Maximizing Earnings and Ensuring Sustainability — 93

7.1 Diversifying Revenue Streams	93
7.1.1 Strategies for Revenue Diversification	93
7.2 Managing Costs and Operational Efficiency	96
7.2.1 Cost Management Strategies	96
7.3 Building Long-Term Sustainability	99
7.3.1 Strategic Sustainability Practices	99
7.4 Strategic Expansion and Future Growth	102
7.4.1 Expansion Strategies	103
Conclusion: Securing Success in Online Education	**106**
1. Embracing Online Education Opportunities	106
2. Setting the Foundation for Success	107
3. Implementing Effective Teaching Strategies	107
4. Scaling Your Business for Growth	107
5. Maximizing Earnings and Ensuring Sustainability	108
6. Looking Ahead: Embracing Innovation	108
Take Action Now!	108
Disclaimer	**110**
Limitation of Liability:	110
Professional Advice:	111
External Links and Resources:	111
Copyright Notice:	111
Disclosure:	112
Legal Compliance:	112
Feedback and Contact:	112

Chapter 1

Introduction to Online Tutoring and Teaching

1.1 Overview of Online Tutoring and Teaching

The digital age has revolutionized education, making knowledge more accessible than ever before. Online tutoring and teaching encompass a broad spectrum of educational activities delivered via the internet. This includes one-on-one tutoring sessions, virtual classrooms, self-paced courses, and webinars. These platforms allow educators to reach students from around the world, providing flexible and personalized learning experiences.

Types of Online Education:

- **Synchronous Learning:** Real-time interaction between tutor and student through video conferencing tools.

- **Asynchronous Learning:** Pre-recorded lessons and materials that students can access at their convenience.
- **Blended Learning:** A mix of synchronous and asynchronous methods.

1.1.1 Understanding Asynchronous Learning

Asynchronous learning is a method of instruction where teaching and learning do not occur in real-time. Instead, students engage with course materials on their own schedule, accessing pre-recorded lectures, reading assignments, discussion boards, and other resources whenever it suits them. This approach offers significant flexibility, allowing students to balance their studies with other commitments such as work or family responsibilities.

Key Components of Asynchronous Learning:

- **Pre-Recorded Lectures:** Video or audio recordings that students can watch or listen to at any time.
- **Reading Materials:** Textbooks, articles, and other written resources available for students to read at their convenience.

- **Discussion Boards:** Online forums where students can post questions, share insights, and engage in discussions with peers and instructors.
- **Assignments and Quizzes:** Tasks that students complete on their own time, often with set deadlines.

1.1.2 Benefits of Asynchronous Learning

Asynchronous learning offers several advantages, making it an attractive option for both students and educators.

Flexibility:

- **Self-Paced Learning:** Students can progress through the course materials at their own pace, spending more time on challenging topics and moving quickly through familiar ones.
- **Convenience:** Learners can access materials at any time and from any location, making it easier to fit education into busy schedules.

Accessibility:

- **Diverse Learning Styles:** Asynchronous learning accommodates different learning styles, allowing

students to review materials multiple times and take notes at their own pace.
- **Broad Reach:** This method enables educators to reach a global audience, breaking down geographical barriers and providing access to education for students in remote areas.

Cost-Effectiveness:

- **Reduced Costs:** Without the need for physical classroom space and live instruction, asynchronous courses can be more affordable for both students and institutions.
- **Scalability:** Educators can create content once and use it for multiple cohorts of students, maximizing the return on investment.

1.1.3 Challenges of Asynchronous Learning

While asynchronous learning offers many benefits, it also comes with its own set of challenges that educators need to address.

Student Engagement:

- **Isolation:** Without real-time interaction, students may feel isolated and disconnected from their peers and instructors.
- **Motivation:** Self-paced learning requires a high level of self-discipline and motivation, which can be challenging for some students.

Communication:

- **Delayed Feedback:** Instructors may not be able to provide immediate feedback, potentially slowing down the learning process.
- **Limited Interaction:** The lack of real-time interaction can make it harder to build a sense of community and collaboration among students.

1.1.4 Strategies for Effective Asynchronous Learning

To overcome these challenges and ensure the effectiveness of asynchronous learning, educators can employ various strategies.

Enhancing Engagement:

- **Interactive Content:** Incorporate multimedia elements such as videos, quizzes, and interactive simulations to make learning more engaging.
- **Regular Check-Ins:** Schedule periodic check-ins via email or video conferencing to maintain a connection with students and provide support.

Improving Communication:

- **Timely Feedback:** Provide prompt feedback on assignments and assessments to keep students informed of their progress.
- **Active Discussion Boards:** Encourage active participation in discussion boards by posing thought-provoking questions and moderating discussions regularly.

Supporting Self-Motivation:

- **Clear Guidelines:** Offer clear instructions and deadlines to help students manage their time effectively.
- **Goal Setting:** Encourage students to set personal learning goals and track their progress throughout the course.

1.1.5 Tools for Asynchronous Learning

Several tools and platforms can facilitate asynchronous learning, making it easier for educators to create and deliver high-quality content.

Learning Management Systems (LMS):

- **Moodle:** An open-source LMS that provides a robust platform for creating and managing online courses.
- **Canvas:** A user-friendly LMS that offers a range of features for course creation, student assessment, and communication.

Content Creation Tools:

- **Camtasia:** A screen recording and video editing tool that allows educators to create professional-looking video lectures.
- **H5P:** An open-source tool for creating interactive content such as quizzes, presentations, and interactive videos.

Communication Tools:

- **Slack:** A messaging platform that facilitates communication and collaboration among students and instructors.
- **Padlet:** An online bulletin board that allows students to post notes, images, and links, fostering collaborative learning.

Benefits of Online Tutoring and Teaching:

- **Flexibility:** Educators and students can choose when and where they learn.
- **Accessibility:** Learners from remote areas can access high-quality education.
- **Personalization:** Customized learning plans to suit individual student needs.

1.2 The Growth of Online Education

Online education has seen exponential growth in recent years. According to industry reports, the global online learning market is projected to reach $350 billion by 2025. The COVID-19 pandemic accelerated this trend, with institutions and individuals adopting online methods out of necessity. The demand for online tutors and teachers continues to rise, driven by the need for accessible, flexible learning solutions.

Key Statistics:

- **Enrollment Surge:** Millions of students enrolled in online courses during the pandemic.
- **Diverse Demographics:** Online learners range from school-aged children to adults seeking professional development.
- **Technological Advancements:** Improved internet connectivity and innovative platforms have enhanced the online learning experience.

1.3 Why Consider Online Tutoring and Teaching?

Entering the field of online tutoring and teaching offers numerous advantages. It provides an opportunity to earn a substantial income while enjoying the flexibility of working from home. Moreover, it allows educators to make a significant impact on students' lives by providing them with quality education and personalized support.

Financial Opportunities:

- **Competitive Earnings:** Tutors can set their rates based on expertise and demand.

- **Multiple Income Streams:** Offering various courses and tutoring services.

Personal Fulfillment:

- **Making a Difference:** Helping students achieve their academic goals.
- **Professional Growth:** Continuous learning and skill development.

Chapter 2

Getting Started as an Online Tutor

2.1 Identifying Your Niche and Expertise

Before diving into online tutoring, it's crucial to identify your niche and area of expertise. This will not only help you stand out in a competitive market but also ensure you are passionate about the subject you are teaching.

Steps to Identify Your Niche:

- **Self-Assessment:** List your qualifications, skills, and interests.
- **Market Research:** Explore popular subjects and what students are seeking.
- **Target Audience:** Determine who you want to teach (e.g., KS2 - KS4 students, college students, professionals).

Popular Subjects in Online Tutoring:

- **Academic Subjects:** Math, Science, English, History
- **Languages:** English as a Second Language (ESL), Spanish, French
- **Test Preparation:** SATs, GCSE, TOEFL, IELTS
- **Professional Skills:** Coding, Digital Marketing, Business Management

2.2 Essential Tools and Technologies

To start online tutoring, you'll need to familiarize yourself with the essential tools and technologies that facilitate effective teaching. This includes both hardware and software.

2.2.1 Required Hardware:

- **Computer or Laptop:** A reliable device with a good processor.
- **High-Speed Internet:** Stable and fast connection to avoid disruptions.
- **Webcam and Microphone:** High-quality video and audio for clear communication.
- **Headphones:** To reduce background noise and improve audio clarity.

2.2.2 Recommended Software:

2.2.2.1 Video Conferencing Tools:

- **Zoom:** Zoom is a popular video conferencing tool that offers features such as screen sharing, breakout rooms, and virtual whiteboards. It is widely used for one-on-one tutoring sessions, group classes, and webinars. Zoom's easy-to-use interface and robust security features make it a top choice for educators.
- **Skype:** Skype has been a staple for online communication for years. It supports video calls, voice calls, and instant messaging. Its user-friendly interface and widespread availability make it a good option for online tutoring.
- **Google Meet:** Part of Google Workspace, Google Meet is integrated with other Google services like Google Calendar and Google Drive. It supports video calls and screen sharing, making it suitable for virtual classrooms and tutoring sessions.

2.2.2.2 Learning Management Systems (LMS):

- **Moodle:** Moodle is an open-source LMS that allows educators to create and manage online courses. It offers features such as customizable course content, quizzes, forums, and grading tools. Moodle's flexibility and extensive plugin library make it a powerful tool for online educators.

- **Canvas:** Canvas is a user-friendly LMS that provides tools for course creation, student assessment, and communication. It supports multimedia content, discussion boards, and integrations with other educational tools. Canvas is known for its intuitive design and strong support community.
- **Blackboard:** Blackboard is a comprehensive LMS that offers a range of features for online teaching, including course content management, student engagement tools, and analytics. It is widely used in higher education and offers robust support for instructors and students.

2.2.2.3 Interactive Tools:

- **Whiteboard.fi:** Whiteboard.fi is an online whiteboard tool that allows tutors to create interactive lessons. Students can draw, write, and interact with the whiteboard in real-time, making it an excellent

tool for subjects that require visual explanations, such as math and science.
- **Google Docs:** Google Docs allows real-time document collaboration, making it ideal for group projects, writing assignments, and sharing notes. Its integration with other Google services enhances its functionality and ease of use.
- **Microsoft OneNote:** OneNote is a digital notebook that supports text, images, and multimedia content. It allows tutors to organize lesson plans, create interactive notebooks, and share materials with students.

2.2.2.4 Content Creation Tools:

- **Camtasia:** Camtasia is a screen recording and video editing tool that enables tutors to create professional-quality video lessons. It supports features like annotations, transitions, and quizzes, making it ideal for creating engaging instructional videos.
- **H5P:** H5P is an open-source tool for creating interactive content such as quizzes, presentations, and interactive videos. It integrates with many LMS

platforms and enhances student engagement through interactive elements.
- **Adobe Spark:** Adobe Spark allows tutors to create visually appealing graphics, web pages, and video stories. It is useful for creating course materials, promotional content, and multimedia presentations.

2.2.2.5 Communication Tools:

- **Slack:** Slack is a messaging platform that facilitates communication and collaboration among students and instructors. It supports channels for different topics, direct messaging, and file sharing, making it a versatile tool for virtual classrooms.
- **Discord:** Originally designed for gamers, Discord has become popular in educational settings for its voice, video, and text communication capabilities. It supports creating servers with multiple channels for different subjects or groups.
- **Remind:** Remind is a communication tool specifically designed for education. It allows tutors to send announcements, assignments, and reminders to students and parents. Its focus on educational use

makes it a practical choice for keeping everyone informed and engaged.

2.2.2.6 Assessment Tools:

- **Kahoot!:** Kahoot! is a game-based learning platform that allows tutors to create fun and interactive quizzes. It is particularly effective for engaging students and assessing their understanding in a playful manner.
- **Quizlet:** Quizlet provides tools for creating flashcards, quizzes, and interactive study games. It supports a wide range of subjects and is popular for test preparation and vocabulary building.
- **Socrative:** Socrative is an assessment tool that allows tutors to create quizzes, polls, and exit tickets. It provides real-time feedback and analytics, helping tutors gauge student understanding and adjust their teaching accordingly.

2.3 Setting Up Your Online Tutoring Business

Establishing a professional and attractive online presence is key to attracting students and building your brand.

Creating a Professional Profile:

- **Detailed Bio:** Highlight your qualifications, experience, and teaching philosophy.
- **Profile Picture:** Use a clear, professional headshot.
- **Testimonials and Reviews:** Collect and display feedback from previous students.

2.3.1 Establishing Your Brand

Creating a strong personal brand is essential for standing out in the competitive field of online tutoring and teaching. Your brand represents your identity as an educator and communicates your values, expertise, and the unique benefits you offer to students.

2.3.1.1 Why Branding Matters:

- **Differentiation:** A strong brand differentiates you from other tutors and helps attract your target audience.

- **Trust and Credibility:** A well-defined brand builds trust and credibility with potential students and their parents.
- **Professionalism:** Consistent branding across all platforms conveys professionalism and reliability.

2.3.1.2 Steps to Establish Your Brand:

1. Define Your Unique Selling Proposition (USP): Your USP is what sets you apart from other tutors. It's the unique value you offer to students.

- **Identify Your Strengths:** Consider your qualifications, teaching style, and any specialized knowledge you have.
- **Understand Your Audience:** Identify the specific needs and preferences of your target students.
- **Craft a Compelling Message:** Develop a clear and concise statement that communicates your USP. For example, "Helping high school students excel in math through personalized, engaging lessons."

2. Create a Professional Online Presence: Your online presence is the face of your brand. It includes your website, social media profiles, and any other online platforms where you interact with potential students.

- **Website:** Build a professional website that showcases your services, qualifications, and testimonials. Include a blog to share valuable content and improve your search engine ranking.
    - **Homepage:** Introduce yourself and your services.
    - **About Page:** Share your background, qualifications, and teaching philosophy.
    - **Services Page:** Detail the tutoring services you offer, including subjects, pricing, and packages.
    - **Contact Page:** Provide easy ways for potential clients to get in touch with you.
- **Social Media:** Create profiles on platforms like LinkedIn, Facebook, and Instagram. Use these channels to engage with your audience, share educational content, and promote your services.
    - **LinkedIn:** Share articles, success stories, and professional updates.

- **Facebook:** Create a business page to post updates, share content, and interact with your community.
- **Instagram:** Use visuals to showcase your tutoring sessions, share tips, and connect with students.

3. Develop a Visual Identity: Your visual identity includes your logo, color scheme, typography, and overall design aesthetic. It should be consistent across all your online and offline materials.

- **Logo:** Create a logo that reflects your brand's personality and values. You can hire a professional designer or use online tools like Canva or LogoMaker.
- **Color Scheme:** Choose a color palette that resonates with your target audience and aligns with your brand's message. For example, blue conveys trust and professionalism, while green signifies growth and learning.
- **Typography:** Select fonts that are easy to read and match your brand's tone. Use these consistently in all your materials.

4. Create Valuable Content: Content marketing is a powerful way to establish yourself as an expert and attract potential students. Share valuable, informative, and engaging content that addresses your audience's needs and interests.

- **Blog Posts:** Write articles on topics related to your subject area, study tips, and educational trends. Optimize your posts for search engines to attract organic traffic.
- **Videos:** Create video tutorials, explainer videos, and live Q&A sessions. Share these on your website, YouTube, and social media.
- **E-books and Guides:** Offer free downloadable resources in exchange for email addresses. This helps you build an email list for future marketing efforts.
- **Webinars:** Host live webinars on relevant topics. This positions you as an authority and provides value to your audience.

5. Collect and Showcase Testimonials: Testimonials and reviews from satisfied students and parents are powerful tools for building trust and credibility.

- **Request Feedback:** After completing a tutoring program, ask your students and their parents for

feedback. Make it easy for them by providing a simple feedback form.
- **Display Testimonials:** Feature positive reviews on your website, social media profiles, and marketing materials.
- **Case Studies:** Create detailed case studies that highlight how your tutoring services have helped students achieve their goals.

6. Network and Collaborate: Building a strong network within the education community can enhance your brand's visibility and credibility.

- **Join Professional Organizations:** Become a member of relevant professional associations and participate in their events and forums.
- **Collaborate with Other Educators:** Partner with other tutors, teachers, and educational institutions to offer joint programs and workshops.
- **Attend Conferences and Workshops:** Participate in industry conferences and workshops to stay updated on trends and network with peers.

7. Maintain Consistency: Consistency is key to building a strong brand. Ensure that your messaging, visuals, and interactions are consistent across all platforms.

- **Brand Guidelines:** Create a brand style guide that outlines your visual and messaging standards. Share this with anyone who works on your branding and marketing materials.
- **Regular Updates:** Keep your website, social media profiles, and other online platforms updated with fresh content and information.
- **Engage with Your Audience:** Regularly interact with your audience through comments, messages, and posts. Show your personality and be responsive to inquiries.

2.3.1.3 Case Study: Building a Successful Online Tutoring Brand

Consider the example of "Math Mastery with Ms. Maria," an online tutoring service specializing in math for high school students.

1. **Defining USP:** Ms. Maria highlights her extensive experience as a high school math teacher and her ability to make complex topics easy to understand.
2. **Online Presence:** She creates a professional website with detailed service descriptions, a blog with math tips, and student testimonials. Her LinkedIn profile shares articles and updates on her tutoring services.
3. **Visual Identity:** Ms. Maria designs a clean, modern logo with a blue and white color scheme, reflecting trust and clarity.
4. **Content Creation:** She regularly posts video tutorials on YouTube, writes blog posts on her website, and shares math challenges on Instagram.
5. **Testimonials:** Ms. Maria collects testimonials from students who have improved their grades and features these on her website.
6. **Networking:** She joins the National Council of Teachers of Mathematics (NCTM) and collaborates with local schools to offer joint math workshops.
7. **Consistency:** All her materials follow a consistent style guide, and she maintains regular engagement with her audience on social media and her blog.

Chapter 3

Finding and Attracting Students

3.1 Choosing the Right Platforms

Selecting the right platform to offer your tutoring services can significantly impact your success. Different platforms cater to various subjects and demographics, so it's important to choose one that aligns with your niche and target audience.

Popular Online Tutoring Platforms:

- **VIPKid:** Specializes in teaching English to Chinese students.
- **Chegg Tutors:** Offers a wide range of subjects for K-12 and college students.
- **Wyzant:** Connects students with tutors in various subjects, including test prep and professional skills.
- **Tutor.com:** Provides tutoring services for school subjects, test prep, and more.

Pros and Cons of Each Platform:

- **VIPKid:** High demand for English tutors but requires specific teaching hours.
- **Chegg Tutors:** Flexible scheduling but competitive.
- **Wyzant:** Allows setting your own rates but takes a commission.
- **Tutor.com:** Provides resources and training but may have more rigorous requirements.

3.2 Marketing Yourself

Effective marketing is crucial for attracting students to your online tutoring services. By implementing a comprehensive marketing strategy, you can increase your visibility, reach your target audience, and build a steady stream of clients.

3.2.1 Key Elements of an Effective Marketing Strategy:

1. Identify Your Target Audience: Understanding your target audience is the first step in any marketing strategy. Identify who your ideal students are based on factors like age, academic level, subjects of interest, and learning goals.

- **Demographics:** Consider the age group, educational level, and location of your potential students.
- **Psychographics:** Understand their learning preferences, challenges, and motivations.
- **Behavioral Patterns:** Identify where they spend time online and what kind of content they engage with.

2. Develop a Strong Online Presence: A robust online presence is essential for reaching a wide audience. Utilize various online platforms to showcase your expertise and connect with potential students.

- **Website:** Your website is your primary marketing tool. Ensure it is professional, easy to navigate, and optimized for search engines (SEO).
    - **SEO:** Use relevant keywords in your website content to improve your search engine ranking. For example, if you specialize in math tutoring, include keywords like "online math tutor," "math tutoring services," and "learn math online."
    - **Content Marketing:** Regularly update your blog with articles, tips, and resources related to your tutoring subjects. This can attract

organic traffic and establish you as an authority in your field.

3. Leverage Social Media: Social media platforms are powerful tools for reaching and engaging with your target audience. Choose platforms that align with your audience's preferences.

- **Facebook:** Create a business page to share updates, educational content, and success stories. Join relevant groups and participate in discussions to increase your visibility.
- **Instagram:** Use Instagram to share visual content like infographics, video snippets of your lessons, and student success stories. Use hashtags to reach a broader audience.
- **LinkedIn:** Build a professional profile and share articles, updates, and endorsements. Connect with other educators and potential clients.
- **YouTube:** Create a YouTube channel to share video tutorials, webinars, and Q&A sessions. Optimize your video titles and descriptions with relevant keywords.

4. Content Marketing: Creating valuable content can help attract and retain students. Share your knowledge and expertise through various forms of content.

- **Blog Posts:** Write informative articles on topics related to your subjects. For example, "5 Tips to Master Algebra" or "How to Prepare for SAT Math."
- **Videos:** Produce video tutorials, live sessions, and recorded webinars. Visual content can be more engaging and easier to consume.
- **E-books and Guides:** Offer free downloadable resources in exchange for email addresses. This helps build your email list for future marketing efforts.
- **Podcasts:** Start a podcast discussing educational topics, interviewing experts, and sharing study tips.

5. Email Marketing: Email marketing is a direct way to communicate with potential and existing students. Build an email list and send regular updates, offers, and valuable content.

- **Newsletter:** Create a monthly or bi-weekly newsletter with updates, tips, and promotions.

- **Automated Campaigns:** Set up automated email campaigns to welcome new subscribers, follow up with leads, and re-engage inactive students.
- **Segmentation:** Segment your email list based on interests and behaviors to send targeted messages.

6. Paid Advertising: Investing in paid advertising can help you reach a larger audience quickly. Use targeted ads to attract students who are actively searching for tutoring services.

- **Google Ads:** Create search ads targeting relevant keywords. Use location-based targeting if you offer local services.
- **Facebook Ads:** Use Facebook's detailed targeting options to reach specific demographics. Run ads promoting your services, free resources, or special offers.
- **Instagram Ads:** Utilize Instagram's visual platform for promoting video snippets, success stories, and free webinars.

7. Networking and Partnerships: Building relationships with other educators, institutions, and professionals can expand your reach and credibility.

- **Educational Institutions:** Partner with schools and colleges to offer supplementary tutoring services or workshops.
- **Professional Organizations:** Join professional associations related to your subjects to network and stay updated on industry trends.
- **Collaborations:** Collaborate with other tutors or educational content creators for joint webinars, courses, or content sharing.

8. Online Tutoring Platforms: Listing your services on popular online tutoring platforms can increase your visibility and attract students.

- **Platforms:** Register on platforms like Tutor.com, Wyzant, and Chegg Tutors to reach a broader audience.
- **Profiles:** Create comprehensive profiles with detailed descriptions of your services, qualifications, and testimonials.
- **Reviews:** Encourage your students to leave positive reviews on these platforms to build your credibility.

9. Referrals and Testimonials: Word-of-mouth and positive testimonials are powerful marketing tools. Encourage satisfied students and parents to refer others to your services.

- **Referral Programs:** Offer discounts or free sessions to students who refer new clients.
- **Testimonials:** Request feedback from your students and feature their testimonials on your website and social media.

10. Public Relations: Engage in public relations activities to increase your brand's visibility and credibility.

- **Press Releases:** Share newsworthy updates, such as new course offerings or special achievements, with local media.
- **Guest Blogging:** Write guest posts for popular educational blogs and websites to reach a broader audience.
- **Interviews and Podcasts:** Participate in interviews and podcasts to share your expertise and promote your services.

3.2.2 Case Study: Effective Marketing for Online Tutors

Consider the example of "Science Success with Dr. Smith," an online tutoring service specializing in science subjects for high school and college students.

1. **Target Audience:** Dr. Smith identifies his target audience as high school and college students struggling with science subjects.
2. **Online Presence:** He creates a professional website with SEO-optimized content and a blog featuring articles like "Understanding Chemistry Basics" and "Tips for Acing Biology Exams."
3. **Social Media:** Dr. Smith uses Facebook and Instagram to share video tutorials, student success stories, and science trivia. He joins educational groups on Facebook to engage with potential students.
4. **Content Marketing:** He produces YouTube videos explaining complex science concepts, writes e-books on study tips for science subjects, and starts a podcast discussing the latest in science education.
5. **Email Marketing:** Dr. Smith sends a monthly newsletter with updates, articles, and exclusive offers.

He sets up automated welcome emails for new subscribers.

6. **Paid Advertising:** He runs Google Ads targeting keywords like "online chemistry tutor" and Facebook Ads promoting free introductory sessions.
7. **Networking:** Dr. Smith partners with local schools to offer supplemental tutoring and joins professional organizations like the National Science Teachers Association (NSTA).
8. **Tutoring Platforms:** He lists his services on platforms like Tutor.com, ensuring his profile is detailed and includes positive reviews from students.
9. **Referrals:** He offers a discount to students who refer new clients and prominently features testimonials on his website.
10. **Public Relations:** Dr. Smith writes guest posts for educational blogs, participates in local media interviews, and is a guest on science education podcasts.

By following these strategies, you can effectively market yourself as an online tutor, attract more students, and build a successful tutoring business.

3.3 Networking and Referrals

Building a strong network and leveraging referrals are essential strategies for growing your online tutoring business. Networking helps you connect with potential clients, peers, and educational institutions, while referrals can provide a steady stream of new students through word-of-mouth recommendations.

3.3.1 Networking Strategies:

3.3.1.1 Join Professional Organizations

Becoming a member of professional organizations related to education and your subject area can provide numerous benefits.

- **National Tutoring Association (NTA):** Joining the NTA offers access to professional development resources, networking opportunities, and industry recognition.
- **Subject-Specific Associations:** Organizations like the National Science Teachers Association (NSTA) or the National Council of Teachers of Mathematics

(NCTM) offer specialized resources and networking opportunities.

3.3.1.2 Attend Conferences and Workshops

Participating in educational conferences and workshops can help you stay updated on industry trends, meet peers, and expand your professional network.

- **Educational Conferences:** Events like the International Society for Technology in Education (ISTE) Conference or regional education conferences provide opportunities for learning and networking.
- **Workshops and Webinars:** Attend and participate in workshops and webinars to learn new teaching strategies and connect with other educators.

3.3.1.3 Participate in Online Communities

Engage with online communities and forums where educators, students, and parents discuss educational topics.

- **Social Media Groups:** Join and participate in Facebook groups, LinkedIn groups, and other social media communities related to education and tutoring.

- **Online Forums:** Engage in discussions on platforms like Reddit (e.g., r/education or r/tutoring) and specialized education forums.

3.3.1.4 Collaborate with Other Educators

Building relationships with other tutors, teachers, and educational content creators can lead to collaborative opportunities and mutual referrals.

- **Guest Appearances:** Partner with other educators for joint webinars, guest blog posts, or podcast appearances.
- **Co-Teaching:** Collaborate with another tutor to co-teach a course or offer complementary services.

3.3.1.5 Connect with Local Schools and Institutions

Forming relationships with local schools, colleges, and educational institutions can provide opportunities for referrals and partnerships.

- **Presentations and Workshops:** Offer to conduct free workshops or presentations for students and parents at local schools.

- **Supplemental Programs:** Collaborate with schools to offer supplemental tutoring programs for students needing extra help.

3.3.2 Referral Strategies

3.3.2.1 Create a Referral Program

Encourage your current students and their parents to refer new clients by offering incentives.

- **Discounts and Free Sessions:** Provide a discount on future tutoring sessions or offer a free session for every successful referral.
- **Gift Cards:** Offer gift cards as a reward for referrals that lead to new clients.

3.3.2.2 Collect and Showcase Testimonials

Positive testimonials and reviews from satisfied clients are powerful tools for attracting new students.

- **Request Feedback:** After completing a tutoring program, ask students and parents for feedback. Make it easy by providing a simple feedback form.

- **Display Testimonials:** Feature positive testimonials prominently on your website, social media profiles, and marketing materials.

3.3.2.3 Leverage Online Reviews

Encourage your clients to leave reviews on online tutoring platforms and review sites.

- **Tutoring Platforms:** Request reviews on platforms like Tutor.com, Wyzant, and Chegg Tutors.
- **Google My Business:** If you have a Google My Business listing, ask clients to leave reviews there to improve your local search visibility.
- **Social Media:** Encourage clients to share their positive experiences on social media and tag your profile.

3.3.2.4 Utilize Email Marketing

Stay in touch with current and past students through email marketing, and gently encourage referrals.

- **Newsletter:** Include a referral request in your monthly or bi-weekly newsletter.

- **Automated Follow-Ups:** Set up automated follow-up emails thanking clients for their business and asking for referrals.

3.3.2.5 Provide Exceptional Service

Delivering outstanding tutoring services naturally encourages word-of-mouth referrals.

- **Personalized Learning:** Tailor your tutoring sessions to meet the specific needs and goals of each student.
- **Engagement and Support:** Maintain high levels of engagement and provide ongoing support to ensure student success.

3.3.2.6 Network with Influencers and Thought Leaders

Building relationships with influencers and thought leaders in the education sector can amplify your reach and credibility.

- **Guest Blogging:** Write guest posts for influential education blogs and websites.
- **Podcast Interviews:** Participate in interviews on popular education podcasts.

- **Social Media Collaboration:** Collaborate with education influencers on social media for joint content or shoutouts.

3.3.2.7 Case Study: Successful Networking and Referral Strategies

Consider the example of "Language Learning with Laura," an online tutoring service specializing in language acquisition.

1. **Professional Organizations:** Laura joins the American Council on the Teaching of Foreign Languages (ACTFL) to access resources and networking opportunities.
2. **Conferences and Workshops:** She attends the ACTFL Annual Convention and regularly participates in language teaching workshops and webinars.
3. **Online Communities:** Laura is active in Facebook groups for language teachers and tutors, where she shares resources and engages in discussions.
4. **Collaborations:** She partners with a popular language learning YouTuber for a joint webinar, increasing her visibility.

5. **Local Schools:** Laura offers free workshops on language learning techniques at local high schools, establishing connections with educators and parents.
6. **Referral Program:** She creates a referral program offering a free session for every new student referred, which quickly generates new clients.
7. **Testimonials:** Laura collects glowing testimonials from her students and features them on her website and social media profiles.
8. **Online Reviews:** She encourages satisfied clients to leave reviews on platforms like Wyzant and Google My Business.
9. **Email Marketing:** Laura sends a monthly newsletter with language learning tips and gently asks for referrals in each issue.
10. **Exceptional Service:** By providing personalized and engaging tutoring sessions, Laura ensures that her students succeed and naturally recommend her services to others.

By implementing these networking and referral strategies, you can effectively grow your online tutoring business and build a strong, sustainable client base.

Chapter 4

Creating Effective Online Courses

4.1 Understanding Online Course Design

Online course design involves structuring and organizing course content in a way that promotes learning and engagement in an online environment.

Key Considerations:

- **Learning Objectives:** Clearly define what students will be able to achieve by the end of the course. Objectives should be specific, measurable, achievable, relevant, and time-bound (SMART). *Example:* For a course on "Introduction to Python Programming," a SMART learning objective could be: "Students will be able to write basic Python programs to solve simple computational problems by the end of the course."

- **Content Sequencing:** Organize course materials logically to facilitate progressive learning. Start with foundational concepts before moving on to more complex topics.

  Example: Begin with basic syntax and variables in Python before progressing to loops, functions, and object-oriented programming.

- **Assessment Strategies:** Plan how you will assess student learning throughout the course. Use a mix of formative (e.g., quizzes, exercises) and summative assessments (e.g., final projects, exams) to evaluate understanding.

  Example: Include weekly quizzes to assess understanding of new programming concepts and a final project where students develop a simple application using Python.

- **Engagement Techniques:** Incorporate interactive elements such as videos, simulations, quizzes, and discussions to keep students engaged and enhance learning.

  Example: Use screencasts to demonstrate coding

examples, interactive coding platforms for practice exercises, and discussion forums for students to ask questions and share insights.

4.2 Structuring Your Course Content

The structure of your online course plays a crucial role in guiding students through the learning process and ensuring they grasp key concepts effectively.

Components of Course Structure:

- **Module Organization:** Divide your course into modules or units based on key topics or themes. Each module should have a clear focus and learning objectives.
  Example: In a biology course, modules could cover topics like cell biology, genetics, and ecology.
- **Lesson Design:** Within each module, structure lessons coherently with a clear introduction, main content, and summary. Use headings, subheadings, and bullet points to enhance readability.
  Example: A lesson on cell biology could include sections on cell structure, function, and types.

- **Navigation:** Ensure easy navigation through the course materials. Use a consistent layout and provide clear instructions on how to proceed through the course.
  Example: Use a sidebar menu or a breadcrumb trail to allow students to navigate between modules and lessons easily.
- **Accessibility:** Design course materials to be accessible to all learners, including those with disabilities. Provide alternative formats for content (e.g., transcripts for videos, accessible documents) and use accessible technologies.
  Example: Use closed captions for videos to accommodate students with hearing impairments.

4.3 Developing Engaging Multimedia Content

Multimedia content enhances the learning experience by presenting information in different formats and catering to diverse learning styles.

Types of Multimedia Content:

- **Videos:** Create instructional videos that explain complex concepts visually. Use screencasts, animations, or live demonstrations to engage students.
  Example: Record a series of short videos demonstrating how to solve math problems using different methods.
- **Interactive Simulations:** Use simulations or virtual labs to allow students to explore concepts in a hands-on manner.
  Example: Provide a virtual chemistry lab where students can perform experiments and observe reactions.
- **Infographics and Visual Aids:** Design infographics, charts, and diagrams to summarize information and make complex concepts more digestible.
  Example: Create an infographic illustrating the steps of the scientific method for a biology course.
- **Podcasts and Audio Lectures:** Record audio lectures or podcasts discussing course topics or featuring guest speakers to provide additional insights.
  Example: Invite a guest expert to discuss current trends in economics for an economics course podcast episode.

4.4 Facilitating Online Discussions and Collaboration

Online discussions and collaboration foster a sense of community among students and encourage active participation in the learning process.

Strategies for Facilitating Discussions:

- **Discussion Forums:** Create forums for students to discuss course topics, ask questions, and share insights. Encourage meaningful interactions and provide prompts to stimulate discussion.
  Example: Pose a discussion question about the ethical implications of artificial intelligence for a computer science ethics course.
- **Peer Review:** Incorporate peer review activities where students provide feedback on each other's work. This promotes critical thinking and improves writing and problem-solving skills.
  Example: Have students peer-review draft research papers in a literature course.
- **Live Sessions:** Schedule live webinars or virtual office hours where students can interact with you and

their peers in real-time. Use these sessions for Q&A, discussions, or guest lectures.

Example: Host a live coding session to demonstrate advanced programming techniques and answer student questions in a software development course.

4.5 Assessing Student Learning Effectively

Assessment is crucial for evaluating student progress and understanding. Implement varied assessment methods to cater to different learning styles and measure learning outcomes accurately.

Types of Assessments:

- **Quizzes and Tests:** Use online quizzes and tests to assess understanding of key concepts. Provide immediate feedback to reinforce learning.
  Example: Administer a weekly quiz on vocabulary and grammar in a language course.
- **Projects and Assignments:** Assign projects or assignments that require students to apply knowledge and skills to real-world scenarios.

Example: Task students with creating a marketing plan for a fictional business in a marketing course.

- **Portfolios:** Have students compile portfolios showcasing their best work throughout the course. Portfolios demonstrate growth and mastery of course objectives.

  Example: Require students in an art history course to create a digital portfolio with analyses of famous artworks.

- **Peer and Self-Assessment:** Incorporate peer and self-assessment activities where students evaluate their own or their peers' work against specific criteria.

  Example: Have students peer-assess group presentations based on content, delivery, and creativity.

4.6 Providing Feedback and Support

Timely and constructive feedback supports student learning by identifying strengths and areas for improvement. Create a feedback loop that encourages student engagement and growth.

Effective Feedback Strategies:

- **Timeliness:** Provide feedback promptly after assessments or assignments to guide students while the content is still fresh.
  Example: Return graded quizzes and tests within 48 hours to ensure timely feedback.
- **Constructiveness:** Offer specific feedback that highlights what students did well and areas where they can improve. Use clear, actionable suggestions for enhancement.
  Example: Provide suggestions for improving the structure and clarity of essay writing in a writing course.
- **Individualization:** Tailor feedback to each student's learning style and needs. Consider providing personalized feedback through one-on-one discussions or written comments.
  Example: Schedule virtual office hours to discuss individual progress and address specific questions in a history course.
- **Encouragement:** Use positive reinforcement to motivate students and acknowledge their efforts and achievements.
  Example: Praise students for demonstrating creativity

and critical thinking in solving a problem in a science course.

4.7 Continuous Improvement and Evaluation

Continuous improvement involves assessing course effectiveness, gathering student feedback, and making enhancements based on evaluation results.

Steps for Continuous Improvement:

- **Course Evaluation Surveys:** Administer surveys at the end of each course to gather feedback from students on course content, structure, and teaching methods.
  Example: Use Likert scale questions to assess student satisfaction and open-ended questions for qualitative feedback.
- **Analyzing Student Performance Data:** Review assessment results and analytics to identify trends and areas where students may struggle. Use data to inform instructional decisions.
  Example: Analyze quiz scores to identify topics

where students may need additional support in a mathematics course.

- **Updating Course Materials:** Regularly update course materials based on feedback, new research, or changes in the field to keep content relevant and engaging.
  Example: Revise a computer science course to include the latest programming languages and technologies.
- **Professional Development:** Participate in professional development activities, attend workshops, or pursue certifications to enhance teaching skills and stay current in your field.
  Example: Enroll in a course design workshop to learn new instructional strategies for an online biology course.

4.8 Platforms for Hosting Courses

Choose a platform that suits your needs for hosting and selling your online courses.

Comparison of Course Hosting Platforms:

- **Teachable:** User-friendly, customizable, and supports multimedia content.
- **Udemy:** Large audience, but higher competition and revenue sharing.
- **Coursera:** Ideal for creating professional courses with certificates.

Setting Pricing and Payment Structures:

- **Competitive Pricing:** Research similar courses to set competitive prices.
- **Discounts and Promotions:** Offer limited-time discounts to attract new students.
- **Payment Plans:** Provide options for installment payments or subscription models.

Chapter 5

Delivering High-Quality Instruction

5.1 Best Practices for Online Teaching

Online teaching requires a different approach compared to traditional classroom instruction. Implementing best practices ensures that you create a conducive learning environment and facilitate meaningful interactions with your students.

Key Best Practices:

1. **Establish Clear Expectations:**
    - **Course Syllabus:** Provide a detailed course syllabus outlining course objectives, expectations, grading criteria, and contact information. Ensure students understand what is expected of them throughout the course.

- *Example:* In an English literature course, include information on reading assignments, writing expectations, and participation requirements.

2. **Create a Structured Learning Environment:**
    - **Consistent Schedule:** Maintain a consistent schedule for releasing lectures, assignments, and assessments. This helps students plan their study time effectively.
        - *Example:* Release new course materials every Monday morning and set deadlines for assignments every Friday at midnight.
    - **Organized Course Layout:** Use a clear and intuitive course layout with easy navigation. Organize content into modules or units, and use headings, subheadings, and bullet points for clarity.
        - *Example:* Divide each module into lessons with clearly labeled topics and provide a checklist of tasks for each week.

3. **Utilize Multiple Communication Channels:**

- **Announcements:** Use course announcements to communicate important updates, reminders, and changes in course schedule promptly.
    - *Example:* Send an announcement at the beginning of each week summarizing upcoming assignments and deadlines.
- **Discussion Forums:** Foster interaction among students and with you through discussion forums. Encourage meaningful discussions, pose thought-provoking questions, and provide guidance as needed.
    - *Example:* Start a weekly discussion thread where students share their reflections on assigned readings and respond to each other's posts.
- **Email and Messaging:** Respond to student inquiries promptly via email or messaging tools provided by the learning management system (LMS).
    - *Example:* Set aside specific times each day to check and respond to

student emails to ensure timely communication.

4. **Engage Students Actively:**
   - **Interactive Content:** Use a variety of multimedia and interactive elements such as videos, simulations, quizzes, and polls to engage students and reinforce learning.
     - *Example:* Incorporate short videos demonstrating key concepts or interactive quizzes to assess understanding.
   - **Real-World Applications:** Relate course content to real-world applications and examples to demonstrate relevance and practicality.
     - *Example:* Discuss case studies or current events related to the course topic in a business ethics course.
   - **Active Learning Strategies:** Implement active learning techniques such as problem-solving activities, group projects, and case studies to encourage critical thinking and collaboration.

- *Example:* Assign a group project where students analyze a business case study and present their findings to the class.

5. **Provide Timely and Constructive Feedback:**
   - **Feedback on Assignments:** Provide clear, specific, and constructive feedback on assignments to help students understand their strengths and areas for improvement.
     - *Example:* Use rubrics to evaluate essays and provide feedback on structure, content, and writing style.
   - **Formative Assessments:** Use formative assessments such as quizzes and short assignments to gauge student understanding throughout the course. Provide feedback promptly to guide learning.
     - *Example:* Administer weekly quizzes on vocabulary and grammar in a language course and review results to identify areas needing reinforcement.

6. **Promote Instructor Presence and Engagement:**
   - **Virtual Office Hours:** Schedule regular virtual office hours or one-on-one sessions

where students can ask questions, seek clarification, and discuss course content.
- *Example:* Hold weekly office hours via video conferencing to provide personalized support and academic guidance.
- **Personalized Feedback:** Address students by name in communications and provide personalized feedback that acknowledges their individual contributions and efforts.
  - *Example:* Recognize student achievements in discussion forums or assignments and provide specific feedback on their contributions.

7. **Encourage Collaboration and Peer Interaction:**
   - **Group Projects:** Assign group projects or collaborative assignments that require students to work together to achieve common goals.
     - *Example:* Have students collaborate on a research project in a psychology course and present their findings as a group.

- **Peer Review:** Incorporate peer review activities where students provide feedback on each other's work. Encourage constructive criticism and respect for differing perspectives.
    - *Example:* Ask students to peer-review draft essays in an English composition course and provide feedback based on assigned criteria.

8. **Monitor Student Progress and Intervene When Needed:**
    - **Analytics and Progress Tracking:** Use analytics and progress tracking tools provided by the LMS to monitor student engagement, participation, and performance.
        - *Example:* Review student quiz scores and participation in discussion forums to identify at-risk students who may need additional support.
    - **Early Intervention:** Identify struggling students early and intervene proactively with personalized support, additional resources, or tutoring services.

- *Example:* Reach out to students who have missed assignments or shown a decline in participation to discuss challenges and provide guidance.

9. **Reflect and Adapt Teaching Strategies:**
    - **Course Evaluations:** Administer course evaluations at the end of each term to gather feedback from students on their learning experience, course content, and teaching methods.
        - *Example:* Analyze feedback from course evaluations to identify strengths and areas for improvement in instructional design and delivery.
    - **Professional Development:** Continuously improve your teaching skills through professional development opportunities, workshops, and collaboration with peers.
        - *Example:* Attend a workshop on online course design to learn new strategies for enhancing student engagement and learning outcomes.

5.2 Handling Challenges

Online teaching presents unique challenges that require proactive strategies to mitigate and address effectively. By understanding common challenges and implementing appropriate solutions, educators can ensure a positive learning experience for their students.

5.2.1. Technological Issues:

- **Preparation and Testing:** Before the course begins, ensure all necessary technologies (e.g., video conferencing software, learning management system) are set up and tested for functionality.
    - *Example:* Conduct a technology orientation session at the start of the course to familiarize students with the tools and troubleshoot any issues.
- **Technical Support:** Provide clear instructions and access to technical support resources for students encountering difficulties with technology.
    - *Example:* Include troubleshooting FAQs and contact information for IT support in the course syllabus and on the course website.
- **Alternative Communication Channels:** Have backup communication channels (e.g., email, phone)

in case of disruptions or technical issues with primary communication tools.
- *Example:* Inform students to check their email for updates in case of unexpected downtime of the learning management system.

5.2.2. Student Engagement and Participation:

- **Varied Learning Styles:** Recognize and accommodate diverse learning styles through multimedia content, interactive activities, and collaborative assignments.
    - *Example:* Offer alternative formats for content delivery (e.g., video lectures, text transcripts, audio recordings) to cater to different preferences.
- **Promoting Interaction:** Actively encourage and facilitate student interaction through discussion forums, group projects, and virtual office hours.
    - *Example:* Pose thought-provoking questions in discussion forums to stimulate meaningful discussions among students.

- **Motivation:** Maintain student motivation by highlighting the relevance of course material, setting clear expectations, and providing timely feedback on assignments.
    - *Example:* Showcase real-world applications of concepts and provide opportunities for students to apply their learning in practical scenarios.

5.2.3 Time Management:

- **Structured Schedule:** Establish a structured schedule with clear deadlines for assignments, assessments, and course activities to help students manage their time effectively.
    - *Example:* Provide a course calendar outlining key dates and milestones for the entire term to help students plan their study schedules.
- **Flexibility:** Offer flexibility in assignment deadlines and participation requirements to accommodate students' varying schedules and time zones.
    - *Example:* Allow students to submit assignments within a specified window of

time to account for differences in personal and professional commitments.

- **Time Zone Considerations:** Acknowledge and accommodate students in different time zones by scheduling synchronous sessions at times accessible to all participants.
  - *Example:* Rotate the timing of live sessions to ensure all students have the opportunity to participate regardless of their geographical location.

5.2.4 Assessment Integrity

- **Fair Assessment Practices:** Implement fair and effective assessment strategies that uphold academic integrity while assessing student learning accurately.
  - *Example:* Use proctoring software or alternative assessment methods (e.g., open-book exams, project-based assessments) to deter cheating and promote authentic learning.
- **Clear Expectations:** Clearly communicate assessment expectations, guidelines, and policies

regarding academic honesty and plagiarism to students.
    - *Example:* Include a statement on academic integrity in the course syllabus and review expectations during orientation sessions.
- **Monitoring and Detection:** Monitor student progress and performance throughout the course to detect any irregularities or signs of academic misconduct.
    - *Example:* Review assignment submissions for consistency and conduct follow-up assessments or discussions with students as needed.

5.2.5 Building Community and Support

- **Instructor Presence:** Maintain a strong instructor presence by actively participating in discussions, providing prompt feedback, and demonstrating availability to students.
    - *Example:* Respond to student questions and comments in discussion forums within a specified timeframe to foster a sense of community and support.

- **Peer Support:** Facilitate peer support and collaboration through group activities, peer review assignments, and virtual study groups.
    - *Example:* Assign group projects that require collaboration and encourage students to share resources and support each other's learning.
- **Accessibility and Inclusivity:** Ensure course materials and activities are accessible to all students, including those with disabilities, and accommodate individual needs as necessary.
    - *Example:* Provide alternative formats for course materials (e.g., text transcripts for videos, accessible documents) and use accessible technologies.

5.2.6 Professional Development and Adaptation

- **Continuous Learning:** Engage in ongoing professional development to enhance online teaching skills, stay updated on technological advancements, and adopt best practices.
    - *Example:* Attend workshops, webinars, and conferences focused on online education, instructional design, and student engagement.

- **Adaptation to Feedback:** Solicit feedback from students through course evaluations and adapt teaching strategies based on feedback to improve course delivery and student satisfaction.
    - *Example:* Analyze feedback from course evaluations to identify areas for improvement in content delivery, assessment methods, and interaction with students.
- **Flexibility and Innovation:** Embrace flexibility and innovation in teaching methods and technologies to adapt to evolving student needs and educational trends.
    - *Example:* Experiment with new instructional tools or educational platforms to enhance student engagement and learning outcomes.

Chapter 6

Scaling Your Online Tutoring Business

6.1 Setting Strategic Goals for Scaling

Scaling your online tutoring business requires setting clear strategic goals to guide your growth trajectory effectively.

6.1.1 Key Steps:

1. **Define Your Objectives:**
    - **Expansion Goals:** Identify specific areas where you want to expand your business, such as increasing the number of clients, expanding into new subject areas, or targeting new demographics.
        - *Example:* Set a goal to double the number of students enrolled in your

tutoring programs within the next year.
- **Revenue Targets:** Establish revenue targets and milestones to measure progress towards your financial objectives.
  - *Example:* Aim to achieve a 30% increase in monthly revenue by the end of the current fiscal year.
- **Market Penetration:** Determine your target market segments and geographical regions for expansion based on demand and growth opportunities.
  - *Example:* Plan to enter new international markets by offering language tutoring services in targeted countries.

2. **Develop a Growth Strategy:**
   - **Marketing and Promotion:** Outline strategies to increase brand visibility and attract new clients through targeted marketing campaigns, partnerships, and digital marketing efforts.
     - *Example:* Launch a social media advertising campaign to promote

discounted trial sessions for new students.
- **Service Diversification:** Consider expanding your service offerings by introducing new tutoring programs, specialized courses, or additional educational services.
  - *Example:* Introduce test preparation courses (e.g., SAT, ACT) to cater to high school students preparing for college admissions.
- **Technology Integration:** Invest in scalable technology solutions, such as learning management systems (LMS), virtual classroom platforms, and automated scheduling systems, to streamline operations and accommodate growth.
  - *Example:* Implement an LMS that supports multiple languages and integrates with video conferencing tools for seamless online tutoring sessions.

6.2 Optimizing Operations for Efficiency

Efficient operations are crucial for scaling your online tutoring business while maintaining service quality and profitability.

6.2.1 Operational Strategies:

1. **Workflow Automation:**
   - **Automated Scheduling:** Implement scheduling software to automate session bookings, rescheduling requests, and reminders for students and tutors.
     - *Example:* Use a cloud-based scheduling tool that syncs with tutors' calendars and sends automated notifications to students.
   - **Payment Processing:** Streamline payment processes with secure online payment gateways and automated invoicing to ensure timely payments and financial transparency.
     - *Example:* Integrate a payment processing system that accepts major

credit cards and offers recurring billing options for subscription-based tutoring services.

2. **Scalable Staffing Solutions:**
    - **Tutor Recruitment:** Develop a scalable recruitment strategy to onboard qualified tutors efficiently, considering factors such as subject expertise, teaching experience, and cultural competency.
        - *Example:* Implement an online application portal and standardized interview process to streamline tutor recruitment and selection.
    - **Training and Development:** Provide ongoing training and professional development opportunities to enhance tutors' skills, maintain quality standards, and support their professional growth.
        - *Example:* Offer virtual workshops and webinars on effective online teaching strategies, technology utilization, and student engagement techniques.

3. **Customer Relationship Management (CRM):**

- **Student Management:** Implement a CRM system to centralize student data, track progress, and personalize learning experiences based on individual needs and preferences.
    - *Example:* Use CRM software to segment students by academic level, learning goals, and preferred communication channels for targeted engagement.
- **Feedback and Improvement:** Gather feedback from students and parents through surveys, reviews, and regular check-ins to continuously improve service delivery and satisfaction.
    - *Example:* Conduct quarterly satisfaction surveys to assess client feedback on tutoring sessions, tutor performance, and overall service quality.

6.3 Scaling Through Strategic Partnerships

Strategic partnerships can accelerate growth and enhance your online tutoring business's market reach and capabilities.

6.3.1 Partnership Opportunities:

1. **Educational Institutions:**
   - **School Partnerships:** Collaborate with K-12 schools, colleges, and universities to offer supplemental tutoring programs, exam preparation courses, or specialized subject workshops.
     - *Example:* Partner with a local high school to provide SAT preparation classes for students aiming to improve their test scores.
   - **Corporate Training:** Develop customized tutoring programs for corporate clients, offering professional development courses, language training, or skills enhancement workshops.
     - *Example:* Partner with multinational corporations to deliver language tutoring services for employees

seeking to improve their communication skills.

2. **Online Platforms and Marketplaces:**
   - **Digital Platforms:** Leverage online tutoring marketplaces, educational platforms, and e-learning marketplaces to reach a broader audience of potential students.
     - *Example:* List tutoring services on popular platforms like Udemy, Coursera, or Khan Academy to attract students interested in self-paced learning options.
   - **Affiliate Marketing:** Establish affiliate partnerships with complementary service providers, such as educational software vendors, to cross-promote products and services to shared target audiences.
     - *Example:* Collaborate with an educational software company to offer discounted tutoring services to customers purchasing their software.

3. **Community Engagement:**
   - **Local Partnerships:** Engage with local community organizations, libraries, and youth

centers to offer free or subsidized tutoring sessions as part of community outreach initiatives.

- *Example:* Sponsor educational workshops at a local library to support student learning and promote your tutoring services to families in the community.

6.4 Monitoring and Evaluating Scalability

Monitoring and evaluating scalability involves assessing key performance indicators (KPIs) and adjusting strategies to ensure sustainable growth and operational efficiency.

6.4.1 Evaluation Metrics:

1. **Financial Performance:**
    - **Revenue Growth:** Track revenue trends, profit margins, and client acquisition costs to gauge financial health and identify opportunities for revenue optimization.

- *Example:* Compare quarterly revenue figures and analyze cost-per-acquisition metrics to assess the effectiveness of marketing campaigns.
  - **Cost Management:** Monitor operational expenses, including technology investments, staffing costs, and marketing expenditures, to control costs and improve profitability.
    - *Example:* Conduct a cost-benefit analysis of implementing new technology solutions versus maintaining existing systems to optimize resource allocation.

2. **Customer Satisfaction:**
   - **Client Retention:** Measure student retention rates, customer satisfaction scores, and referral rates to evaluate service quality and customer loyalty.
     - *Example:* Calculate the percentage of returning students and analyze customer feedback to identify areas for service enhancement.

- **Net Promoter Score (NPS):** Survey clients to assess their likelihood of recommending your tutoring services to others and use NPS scores to gauge overall customer advocacy.
    - *Example:* Implement regular NPS surveys and benchmark scores against industry standards to benchmark customer satisfaction levels.

3. **Operational Efficiency:**
    - **Scalability Assessment:** Assess the scalability of your tutoring model by evaluating the capacity to accommodate increasing demand, expand service offerings, and enter new markets.
        - *Example:* Conduct scenario planning exercises to simulate business growth scenarios and identify potential operational bottlenecks.
    - **Technology Performance:** Monitor the performance of technological infrastructure, including LMS functionality, server reliability, and data security measures, to ensure scalability and data integrity.

- *Example:* Conduct regular system audits and performance tests to identify vulnerabilities and optimize platform performance for increased user traffic.

Chapter 7

Maximizing Earnings and Ensuring Sustainability

7.1 Diversifying Revenue Streams

Diversifying revenue streams is essential for maximizing earnings and reducing dependency on a single source of income.

7.1.1 Strategies for Revenue Diversification

1. **Tutoring Services**
   - **Subject Specialization:** Offer specialized tutoring services in high-demand subjects or niche topics to attract a broader range of students.
     - *Example:* Provide advanced mathematics tutoring for high school

and college students preparing for standardized tests.
- **Test Preparation:** Develop test preparation courses for standardized exams (e.g., SAT, ACT, GRE) to cater to students seeking admission to educational institutions.
  - *Example:* Design intensive SAT preparation classes with personalized study plans and mock exams for comprehensive exam readiness.

2. **Subscription Services:**
   - **Monthly Packages:** Introduce subscription-based tutoring packages that offer students discounted rates for recurring sessions or access to exclusive study materials.
     - *Example:* Offer a monthly subscription plan for unlimited access to tutoring sessions in a specific subject area or academic level.
   - **Membership Programs:** Create membership programs with tiered pricing structures, offering additional benefits such as priority scheduling, bonus sessions, or access to specialized workshops.

- *Example:* Launch a VIP membership program for students and parents, including personalized tutoring plans and priority support from dedicated tutors.

3. **Group Classes and Workshops:**
   - **Group Tutoring Sessions:** Organize group tutoring classes for small cohorts of students with similar learning objectives, maximizing tutor efficiency and student interaction.
     - *Example:* Conduct weekly group sessions in foreign language tutoring, focusing on conversation practice and cultural immersion.
   - **Skill-Based Workshops:** Offer skill-based workshops in areas such as writing, public speaking, or STEM subjects to attract learners seeking targeted skill development.
     - *Example:* Host weekend workshops on coding fundamentals for beginners, combining theory with hands-on programming exercises.

7.2 Managing Costs and Operational Efficiency

Effective cost management is crucial for maintaining profitability and sustainability in your online tutoring business.

7.2.1 Cost Management Strategies

1. **Technology Investments:**
   - **Cloud-Based Solutions:** Utilize cloud-based platforms and software for tutoring sessions, content delivery, and administrative tasks to reduce infrastructure costs.
     - *Example:* Adopt a cloud-based learning management system (LMS) for storing course materials, tracking student progress, and facilitating communication.
   - **Telecommunication Tools:** Invest in reliable video conferencing tools and communication technologies to enhance virtual tutoring sessions and minimize travel expenses.

- *Example:* Use a secure video conferencing platform with interactive features for engaging online tutoring sessions.

2. **Operational Efficiency:**
   - **Workflow Automation:** Implement automated scheduling systems, payment processing tools, and administrative workflows to streamline operations and reduce manual tasks.
     - *Example:* Integrate an automated scheduling software that syncs with tutors' availability and sends session reminders to students.
   - **Outsourcing Non-Core Activities:** Consider outsourcing non-core functions such as accounting, IT support, or marketing to specialized service providers to lower operational costs.
     - *Example:* Partner with a virtual assistant service to handle administrative tasks such as email management and customer inquiries.

3. **Supplier Negotiations:**

- **Vendor Relationships:** Negotiate competitive pricing and favorable terms with suppliers, including educational resources, software licenses, and tutoring materials.
    - *Example:* Establish long-term partnerships with textbook publishers to access discounted rates on educational materials for tutoring sessions.
- **Bulk Purchasing:** Optimize procurement processes by purchasing supplies, equipment, and software licenses in bulk to benefit from volume discounts and reduce per-unit costs.
    - *Example:* Buy classroom supplies and teaching aids in bulk quantities to lower unit costs and ensure sufficient inventory for tutoring sessions.

7.3 Building Long-Term Sustainability

Building long-term sustainability involves strategic planning, continuous improvement, and adapting to market trends to ensure business longevity.

7.3.1 Strategic Sustainability Practices

1. **Market Research and Trends Analysis:**
    - **Industry Insights:** Stay informed about industry trends, educational reforms, and technological advancements to anticipate market shifts and adapt your tutoring services accordingly.
        - *Example:* Conduct regular market research surveys and competitor analysis to identify emerging trends in online education and tutoring preferences.
    - **Student Demographics:** Understand the demographic profiles, learning preferences, and behavioral patterns of your target audience to tailor tutoring programs and marketing strategies.
        - *Example:* Analyze student feedback and enrollment data to identify demographic trends and adjust tutoring offerings to meet evolving student needs.

2. **Continuous Learning and Professional Development:**
    - **Educator Training:** Invest in ongoing training and development programs for tutors to enhance teaching skills, stay updated on curriculum changes, and adopt innovative instructional methods.
        - *Example:* Provide tutors with access to professional development workshops, webinars, and certifications in specialized tutoring techniques.
    - **Industry Certifications:** Obtain industry certifications or accreditations to validate the quality of your tutoring services and enhance credibility with students, parents, and educational institutions.
        - *Example:* Earn certification from recognized organizations in online education or subject-specific tutoring areas to demonstrate expertise and commitment to excellence.
3. **Client Relationship Management (CRM):**

- **Customer Loyalty Programs:** Implement customer loyalty initiatives, rewards programs, or referral incentives to foster long-term relationships and encourage repeat business.
    - *Example:* Offer discounts on tutoring packages for returning students and their referrals as a gesture of appreciation for their loyalty and support.
- **Feedback Mechanisms:** Solicit feedback from students and parents through satisfaction surveys, reviews, and focus groups to assess service quality and identify opportunities for improvement.
    - *Example:* Conduct periodic feedback sessions with clients to gather insights on tutoring experiences, learning outcomes, and areas for enhancement.

7.4 Strategic Expansion and Future Growth

Strategic expansion involves seizing growth opportunities, expanding market reach, and diversifying service offerings to capitalize on emerging trends in online education.

7.4.1 Expansion Strategies

1. **Geographical Expansion:**
   - **Regional Markets:** Explore opportunities to enter new geographical markets or expand operations into underserved regions with high demand for tutoring services.
     - *Example:* Launch localized marketing campaigns targeting specific cities or regions to raise awareness and attract new students.
   - **International Markets:** Consider international expansion by offering online tutoring services to students globally, leveraging technology to overcome geographical barriers.
     - *Example:* Partner with international schools or language institutes to provide English language tutoring services to students abroad.

2. **Vertical Integration:**
   - **Vertical Expansion:** Expand vertically by diversifying into related educational services such as academic counseling, career coaching, or specialized subject workshops.
     - *Example:* Introduce college admissions consulting services to assist high school students with university applications and interview preparation.
   - **Cross-Selling Opportunities:** Cross-sell complementary products or services, such as educational resources, tutoring materials, or online courses, to maximize revenue from existing clients.
     - *Example:* Offer discounted rates on tutoring sessions for clients purchasing educational books or digital learning resources through your online store.
3. **Strategic Partnerships and Alliances:**
   - **Industry Collaborations:** Form strategic partnerships with educational institutions, corporate entities, or online platforms to

expand reach, access new client bases, and enhance service offerings.

- *Example:* Collaborate with a digital learning platform to integrate tutoring services into their educational content offerings for enhanced user engagement.

o **Affiliate Marketing Programs:** Establish affiliate marketing programs with industry influencers, bloggers, or educational content creators to promote your tutoring services and drive referral traffic.

- *Example:* Partner with popular education bloggers to feature guest posts or sponsored content promoting your tutoring programs to their audience.

Conclusion: Securing Success in Online Education

Congratulations on reaching the conclusion of this comprehensive guide to making money through online tutoring and teaching! Throughout this e-book, we've explored essential strategies and actionable insights designed to help you establish, grow, and sustain a successful online tutoring business. Let's recap the key principles and takeaways:

1. Embracing Online Education Opportunities

In today's digital age, online education presents limitless opportunities for educators and tutors to reach students globally. By leveraging technology and innovative teaching methods, you can deliver personalized learning experiences that cater to diverse student needs and preferences.

2. Setting the Foundation for Success

Establishing a solid foundation is crucial for the success of your online tutoring business. From defining your niche and identifying your target audience to creating a compelling brand and designing effective courses, every step plays a pivotal role in attracting and retaining students.

3. Implementing Effective Teaching Strategies

Effective teaching goes beyond subject knowledge; it involves engaging students, fostering interaction, and providing meaningful feedback. By adopting best practices in online teaching, such as utilizing multimedia resources, promoting active learning, and maintaining a supportive learning environment, you can enhance student engagement and learning outcomes.

4. Scaling Your Business for Growth

Scaling your online tutoring business requires strategic planning and proactive measures to expand your reach, diversify revenue streams, and optimize operational efficiency. Whether through partnerships, diversified service offerings, or leveraging technological advancements, scaling enables you to maximize earnings while ensuring sustainability in a competitive market.

5. Maximizing Earnings and Ensuring Sustainability

To maximize earnings and ensure long-term sustainability, effective cost management, continuous learning, and client relationship management are essential. By diversifying revenue streams, managing costs efficiently, and building strong client relationships, you can strengthen your business's financial health and resilience against market fluctuations.

6. Looking Ahead: Embracing Innovation

As the landscape of online education continues to evolve, staying adaptable and embracing innovation will be key to sustaining success. Keep abreast of industry trends, technological advancements, and student preferences to continually enhance your offerings and maintain a competitive edge.

Take Action Now!

Armed with the knowledge and strategies outlined in this e-book, it's time to take action towards building and growing your online tutoring business. Whether you're a seasoned educator or just starting out, remember that every step you take towards improving your teaching, expanding your reach, and enhancing student experiences contributes to your success.

Start by:

- **Implementing Key Strategies:** Choose one or two strategies from each chapter to focus on initially, ensuring you have a solid foundation before scaling further.
- **Seeking Continuous Improvement:** Stay open to feedback, adapt to changes in the educational landscape, and continuously refine your approach to teaching and business management.
- **Building Relationships:** Cultivate strong relationships with students, parents, fellow educators, and industry partners to foster trust, loyalty, and collaboration.

Remember, your journey towards success in online tutoring and teaching is a continuous learning experience.

Thank you for embarking on this journey with us. We wish you all the best in your endeavors to make a meaningful impact through online education!

Disclaimer

The information provided in this e-book, "Making Money Through Online Tutoring and Teaching," is intended for educational and informational purposes only. The content is based on research, experience, and best practices in the field of online education and tutoring.

Limitation of Liability:

While every effort has been made to ensure the accuracy and completeness of the information presented, the authors and publishers do not guarantee the efficacy, applicability, or suitability of the strategies and recommendations discussed. Readers are advised to use their discretion and judgment when implementing any advice or techniques from this e-book.

Professional Advice:

This e-book does not constitute professional advice, legal advice, or financial advice. Readers should seek professional consultation or advice specific to their individual circumstances and needs before making any decisions or taking actions related to starting or operating an online tutoring business.

External Links and Resources:

References to third-party websites, tools, or resources are provided for convenience and informational purposes. The authors and publishers do not endorse, control, or take responsibility for the content, accuracy, or availability of external sites linked within this e-book.

Copyright Notice:

All content, including text, images, and illustrations, in this e-book is protected by copyright law. Reproduction, distribution, or unauthorized use of any part of this e-book without permission from the authors or publishers is strictly prohibited.

Disclosure:

The authors may have financial interests or receive compensation from certain products, services, or companies mentioned in this e-book. However, any such affiliations are disclosed to maintain transparency and do not influence the content or recommendations provided.

Legal Compliance:

Readers are responsible for ensuring compliance with local laws, regulations, and licensing requirements applicable to online tutoring businesses in their jurisdiction.

Feedback and Contact:

We welcome feedback, suggestions, and inquiries regarding this e-book. Please contact us at [info@deservetuition.com] for any questions or clarifications.

About The Authors

Robert Musimbago is a scientist who graduated with a Bachelor of Pharmacy from Makerere University and a MSc. Pharmaceutical Engineering from the University of Sheffield in the United Kingdom, Robert works in Pharmaceutical manufacturing with Big Pharma companies in the UK and has for over 5 years worked along with his wife Ruth K. Musimbago is running a family business which offers tuition services. On the other hand Ruth is a professional teacher and she holds a BSc. Education, Biology Chemistry and a MSc. Public Health from Salford University in the United Kingdom. Ruth works part time as a science teacher in schools in Cambridge UK. They chose to share these ideas with anyone interested in tutoring as a business. "We hope you find this information helpful".

www.ingramcontent.com/pod-product-compliance
Lightning Source LLC
Chambersburg PA
CBHW071940210526
45479CB00002B/752